D1456458

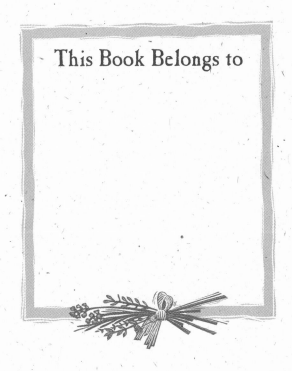

This Book Belongs to

The mission of Storey Communications is to serve our customers
by publishing practical information that encourages personal independence
in harmony with the environment.

Edited by Pamela Lappies
Cover and interior illustrations by Mary Rich
Design and production by Meredith Maker
Production assistance by Susan Bernier
Indexed by Northwind Editorial Services

Some recipes have been adapted from other Storey Publishing books: page 18: *Herbal Treasures* by Phyllis V. Shaudys; page 19: *Mushroom Cookery* by Jo Mueller; page 26: *Satisfying Soups* by Phyllis Hobson; page 46: *Picnic!* by Edith Stovel; page 51: *Surprising Citrus* by Audra and Jack Hendrickson; page 56: *The Carrot Cookbook* by Audra and Jack Hendrickson; page 57: *The Joy of Gardening Cookbook* by Janet Ballantyne.

The information in this book is true and complete to the best of our knowledge. All recommendations are made without guarantee on the part of the author or Storey Communications, Inc. The author and publisher disclaim any liability in connection with the use of this information. For additional information please contact Storey Communications, Inc., Schoolhouse Road, Pownal, Vermont 05261.

Printed in Canada by Métropole Litho

10 9 8 7 6 5 4 3 2 1

**Library of Congress
Cataloging-in-Publication Data**

Bass, Ruth, 1934–
     Herbal soups / Ruth Bass; illustrated by
     Mary Rich.
          p.   cm.
     "A fresh-from-the-garden cookbook."
     ISBN 0-88266-924-9 (hc : alk. paper)
     1. Soups.   2. Cookery (Herbs)
        3. Herbs.   I. Title.
TX757.B373
641.8'13—dc20   96-150
                                                      CIP

HeRBAL SOUPs

A
Fresh from the Garden
Cookbook

RUTH BASS

ILLUSTRATED BY MARY RICH

STOREY

A Storey Publishing Book
Storey Communications, Inc.

Introduction

Built at the turn of the century by a rich American who wanted to duplicate a Scottish castle, Blantyre in Lenox, Massachusetts, is a handsome, dark building of brick and stone.

Today Blantyre is a luxury hotel with a gourmet restaurant. In addition to its sumptuous meals, fine wine cellar, beautiful grounds, and handsomely restored dining rooms and lobby, it has one feature that most guests taste but probably don't see — an extensive herb garden not far from the kitchen door.

The garden, compact and packed, reflects two quite different traditions. It has design, like the elegant herb gardens of England and Europe, with plants placed along mini-walks and against the walls in an eye-appealing way. But it is as utilitarian as the kitchen gardens that America's colonial housewives kept just beyond their back doors. These were the places where, in raised beds and in simple rows or clumps, they cultivated herbs for both medicinal and culinary purposes.

Blantyre's garden boasts more than 30 herbs — including lemon thyme, lemon verbena, lavender, savory, blue balsam mint, sweet woodruff, and eucalyptus. But its real beauty is that as you step carefully along the tiny stone and gravel paths among the many herbs, you see strong evidence that much of this greenery is not growing in landscaped perfection. It has been plucked for cooking. Tops are clipped, sometimes nearly to the ground.

Blantyre's chef, Michael Roller, takes pride in the aesthetics of the garden, but he also uses it. He is a strong advocate of having herbs at the door. Because they are at hand, he says he experiments more with herbs and has even tried them in his creme caramel.

When winter frosts the Berkshire Hills, Chef Roller has the bay-leaf tree and the eucalyptus taken inside. To avoid a deficit in the kitchen when the garden is dormant, he makes many of the herbs into purees that can be stored for some time in the refrigerator or frozen for longer periods. When he needs to pop some freshness into a soup or other dish, the harvest is available.

Anyone with space for a garden can follow Chef Roller's example. Basil, any kind of parsley, dill, chervil, and garlic are easy to add to the vegetable garden. Borage, lavender, savory, rosemary, oregano, and chives — all perennials — can be added to a flower garden or tucked into the crevices of a rock garden.

Chives reappear so early that they are a cook's harbinger of spring. And the blossoms of oregano, lavender, chives, and borage are not only good for garnishes but are also attractive.

For those who have no garden space, containers on the deck or patio can hold some herbs, as long as their needs for water and sun are met. A strawberry jar in rosy ceramic is a perfect place to plant small herbs like creeping thyme or rosemary or even parsley and chives, since those will get a haircut pretty often. Fresh herbs are plentiful these days in the supermarket, but how much better to harvest them outside the door, unsprayed and picked just minutes before they hit the pot.

5

Herbs for Soup, Sauces, and Casseroles

When the basil leaves are glossy and unmarred by insects, when the parsley is fluffy and the dill at its feathery best, save some for winter, just as you would peaches or green beans. Made into pastes and stored in the freezer, herbs can be added to soups, casseroles, and sauces. Unless you are sure you want a given combination of herbs, do them separately. You can always combine a lump of basil and a lump of parsley later.

With a little experimenting on quantity, these pastes can be substituted for most of the herb requirements in this book — in the Zucchini Soup, for instance, or instead of the parsley and thyme in the Minestrone, or in Summer Carrot Soup when it's no longer summer. A collection of pastes makes the variety of Pasta in Brodo almost limitless.

If fresh herbs aren't available and you must use dried, substitute half the quantity indicated for fresh.

1 large bunch cilantro, sage, rosemary, mint, tarragon,
*   basil, marjoram, dill, or oregano (about 2 cups chopped)*
⅓ cup extra-virgin olive oil

1. Line a cookie sheet with wax paper.
2. In a food processor, coarsely chop fresh herb leaves.
3. Add oil through the top while the motor is still running.
4. Drop tablespoonfuls of the herb paste on the cookie sheet. Cover with a layer of plastic wrap and freeze.
5. When the mounds are solid, place them in plastic bags, seal, and store in the freezer. An ice cube tray can also be used, as long as it's the easy-release type.

12–20 TABLESPOONFULS

Cream of Asparagus Soup

When the first asparagus, shaped like rosy pencils, push their way through the soil in spring, it ought to be a holiday. Once the appetite for piles of steamed stalks with butter and black pepper has been appeased, it's time for soup.

> 8–10 asparagus spears, steamed gently until soft
> 1 onion, thinly sliced
> 1 cup asparagus water, reserved from the cooking
> 1½ cups water
> 2 tablespoons butter
> 2 tablespoons flour
> 2 tablespoons minced fresh parsley
> Salt and freshly ground pepper
> 1 cup milk or light cream, warmed
> 1 teaspoon capers

1. After steaming the asparagus, cut off the tips and set aside. Combine the asparagus stalks, onion, asparagus water, and plain water in a soup pot and boil for about 5 minutes.
2. Place the mixture in a blender or food processor and puree.

3. Melt the butter. Add the flour and stir until blended. Blend in the parsley and then whisk in the soup puree. Cook about 5 minutes, stirring.
4. Add salt and pepper to taste, and the warm milk or cream. Put the reserved asparagus tips in soup cups and pour the hot soup over them. Garnish with capers.

4 SERVINGS

Marjoram will attract bees to the garden.

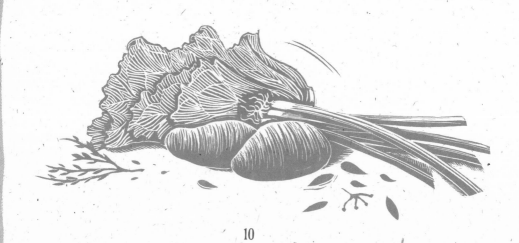

Watercress Soup

Watercress — as cool as the chilly waters where it likes to grow — has a nice bite to it. The potatoes add body to this creamy soup.

3–4 potatoes, peeled and cubed (about 2 cups)
2 bunches watercress, washed carefully and finely chopped
2 large white onions, cut into chunks
6 cups water, slightly salted
2 egg yolks
½ cup milk or light cream
¼ cup dry white wine
Salt and freshly ground pepper
2 garlic cloves, sliced in half
2 tablespoons minced fresh marjoram

1. In a large saucepan, combine the potatoes, watercress, and onions. Cover with the water. Simmer for 30 to 45 minutes over medium heat, or until the potatoes are soft.
2. Put the mixture in a food processor and puree. Return the mixture to the soup pot and heat almost to the boiling point.
3. Beat the egg yolks and milk or light cream until smooth. Stir into the soup. Add the wine, and season with salt and pepper to taste.
4. Rub soup bowls with garlic before adding soup. Garnish with the marjoram.

6 SERVINGS

Herbed Spinach Soup

Green and good, this soup has the bite of sorrel and fresh scallions. Its thickness comes from the potatoes.

4 tablespoons butter
8 ounces fresh spinach, finely chopped (about 1 cup)
4 ounces fresh sorrel, chopped (about ½ cup)
1 small head lettuce, shredded
3 scallions, white part only, shredded
4 medium potatoes, chopped
2 quarts boiling water
1 tablespoon chopped fresh chervil
Salt and freshly ground pepper

1. In a large soup pot, melt the butter and add the spinach, sorrel, lettuce, and scallions. Simmer for 15 minutes, stirring occasionally.
2. Add the potatoes and boiling water to the pot. Simmer, covered, for 45 minutes.
3. Remove the potatoes, mash them, and return them to the pot, along with the chervil. Simmer for 5 minutes. Add salt and pepper to taste before serving. Do not freeze.

2 QUARTS

12

Pasta in Brodo

For the very simplest pasta soup, put leftover noodles into a warmed soup bowl and fill the bowl with hot, canned tomato soup. One step beyond that is this easy-to-make, but homemade, soup with orzo.

2 quarts clear chicken broth
1 tablespoon minced sweet onion
2 carrots, finely chopped
2 stalks celery, thinly sliced
2 garlic cloves, minced
4 tablespoons orzo noodles, uncooked
2 tablespoons finely chopped Italian parsley
3 scallions, cut in 1-inch pieces and shredded

1. Heat the broth. Add the onion, carrots, celery, and garlic, and simmer, covered, for about 20 minutes.
2. In another pan, cook the orzo according to package instructions until it is al dente. Drain and stir into the soup along with the finely chopped parsley.
3. Simmer the soup for 4 minutes, uncovered. Pour into preheated soup bowls with the shreds of scallions floating on top.

4 SERVINGS

Garlic Soup

It's a bit of trouble to make this soup — roasting the garlic separately and then popping it out of its peel and into the soup — but the result is a wonderfully garlicky potion.

> 5 heads of garlic (3 unseparated; 2 separated into
>   cloves and peeled)
> 4 tablespoons extra virgin olive oil
> ½ teaspoon salt
> Freshly ground pepper
> 2 sweet white onions, peeled and chopped
> ¾ pound shallots, peeled and chopped
> 1 pound potatoes, peeled and coarsely diced
> 4 cups chicken broth
> 1 cup light cream
> 1 tablespoon chopped fresh thyme
> 2 tablespoons chopped fresh Italian parsley

1. In a small casserole, toss the unseparated garlic heads in half the oil with the salt and the pepper to taste. Cover and bake at 350°F for 35 minutes, or until the garlic is soft when pricked with a toothpick. Set aside to cool.

2. Heat the remaining oil in a soup pot, and cook the onions slowly until soft and golden. Add the peeled garlic and the shallots; cook another 10 minutes. Add the potatoes, broth, cream, thyme, and parsley. Simmer about 25 minutes.

3. Cut the roasted garlic heads in half and squeeze out the garlic cloves from the skins. Puree the roasted garlic in a blender and add to the soup. Cook another 10 minutes and season with additional salt and pepper to taste.

4. If the soup is too thick, add more chicken broth or a little skim milk. Reheat gently before serving.

6 SERVINGS

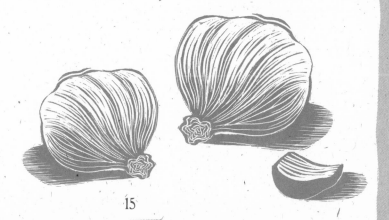

Hot and Sour Soup

The variety of ingredients, some unfamiliar, in this soup prompted one guest to fish each one out individually and demand identification. The blending of textures and flavors, with the added bite of fresh cilantro, is extraordinary.

PORK MARINADE

- 1   teaspoon soy sauce
- 1   teaspoon white wine
- 3   teaspoons cornstarch
- 2   teaspoons sesame oil

SOUP INGREDIENTS

- ¼   pound pork, boneless
- 1   tablespoon Chinese tree ears
- 16   tiger lily buds
- 5   medium-size shiitake mushrooms
- 2   tablespoons tofu
- 2   tablespoons cornstarch
- 3   tablespoons cold water
- 1   egg

- 1   teaspoon sesame oil
- 1½   tablespoons soy sauce
- 2   tablespoons red wine vinegar
- Freshly ground pepper
- 1   teaspoon hot chili oil
- 4   cups chicken broth
- 2   teaspoons minced fresh cilantro

1. Cut the pork into ¼-inch slices. Stack the slices and shred them. Place the pork in a bowl and marinate with the soy sauce, white wine, cornstarch, and oil. Refrigerate.
2. Soak the tree ears and tiger lily buds in separate bowls of warm water until expanded and soft.
3. Rinse the tree ears and tiger lily buds. Remove the tough stems of the tree ears and the knobby ends of the lily buds. Shred both in the same manner as the pork. Thinly slice the shiitake mushrooms and cut into 1-inch lengths.
4. Cut the tofu into 2-inch pieces, ¼-inch thick.
5. Dissolve the cornstarch in a small bowl with the cold water. Beat the egg with the sesame oil in a separate bowl.
6. Combine the soy sauce, red wine vinegar, black pepper to taste, and hot chili oil and place in a serving bowl.
7. In a large soup pot, bring the broth to a boil. Add the shiitake mushrooms and tiger lily buds. Reduce the heat and simmer about 5 minutes. Add the pork, bring to a boil, and add the tree ears and tofu. Reduce the heat again and simmer 5 minutes.
8. Stir the cornstarch mixture and add to the soup slowly, stirring constantly. Pour the beaten egg in wide circles over the surface of the soup, breaking up the resulting ribbons with a spoon.
9. Pour the hot soup into the serving bowl containing the soy sauce mixture and sprinkle the cilantro over the top.

6–8 SERVINGS

Creamy Potato Soup

Sometimes potatoes are just an aside in a soup. In this case, they take center stage and play the part perfectly.

3 pounds potatoes	2 teaspoons freshly ground pepper
2 quarts water	2 tablespoons butter
1 teaspoon salt	1 cup plain yogurt
1 large sweet onion, chopped	¼ cup chopped fresh Italian parsley
1½ tablespoons finely snipped	or cilantro for garnish
fresh dill	

1. Wash and peel the potatoes and cut into cubes. In a large pot, cover them with salted water and bring them to a boil. Reduce the heat and simmer for 10 minutes.
2. Add the onion and simmer for another 10 minutes or until the potatoes start to fall apart. Add the dill, pepper, butter, and yogurt, one at a time, stirring each into the soup. Bring back to a simmer and serve, garnished with parsley or, for a spikier taste, a bit of cilantro. If the soup is too thick, add a little warm milk.

4 SERVINGS

Mushroom Barley Soup

The relationship between a fresh mushroom and a canned one is distant, almost as far as the space between garlic powder and freshly pressed garlic cloves. Here's an old-fashioned mushroom soup with a fresh taste.

> ½ pound fresh mushrooms, sliced
> 2 onions, diced
> 4 tablespoons butter
> ½ cup pearl barley
> 3 teaspoons minced fresh marjoram
> 2 quarts water
> Salt and freshly ground pepper
> 2 tablespoons flour
> 1 cup milk or light cream

1. Sauté the mushrooms and onions in the butter for 5 minutes without browning.
2. Add the barley, marjoram, water, and salt and pepper to taste. Simmer for about an hour over low heat.
3. Mix the flour with the milk or cream and stir into the soup. Heat thoroughly without boiling and stir until slightly thickened.

6 SERVINGS

19

Chili Pepper Soup

Some soup is hot to the touch. Some soup is even hotter to the palate. This one is both. It's for the adventurous, not those who prefer a clear broth with a little rice. Keep in mind that a habanero pepper is 1,000 times hotter than a jalapeño, and choose accordingly.

4–8 dried chili peppers
2 quarts milk
Large sprig of fresh rosemary
2 tablespoons whole coriander seeds
2 bay leaves
1 jalapeño or habanero pepper, seeded
4 tablespoons butter
2 sweet white onions, coarsely chopped
1 teaspoon salt
4 large garlic cloves, minced
2 teaspoons ground cumin
8 cups corn kernels, fresh if possible (otherwise,
     dry-pack canned)
Chives for garnish, finely snipped

1. Soak the dried chili peppers in warm water for 2 hours. Drain them, pat dry, split, remove the seeds, and chop.
2. In a saucepan, combine the milk, rosemary, coriander seeds, bay leaves, and hot pepper. Cook over low heat until it is just starting to simmer. Remove from heat and let stand, covered, for 15 minutes.
3. Melt the butter in a large pot over medium heat. Add the onions and salt and cook gently until golden. Add the garlic and cumin. Cook, stirring, until the cumin gives off its aroma.
4. Stir in the corn and chopped chili peppers and cook over low heat for another 5 minutes.
5. Strain the herb-flavored milk into the corn mixture and simmer for about 15 minutes. Puree about a third of the soup in a blender and return it to the pot.
6. Taste and correct the seasonings. Serve hot, garnished with a sprinkle of chives.

8 SERVINGS

Fish Chowder

Asked what kind of fish was in her delicious chowder, a Nova Scotia fisherman's wife answered that she just went to the freezer and took out whatever was available. The fish chunks were all very white, and the broth was white and sweet, something like this filling soup.

1½ pounds white fish fillets
2 cups water
3 medium potatoes
2 scallions
¼ cup diced salt pork
1 onion, chopped
1 teaspoon chopped fresh thyme
½ cup chopped fresh parsley
3 cups milk
1 tablespoon chopped fresh tarragon
Salt and freshly ground pepper

1. Cut the fish into chunks and put it in a pot with the water. Simmer over medium heat for 3 or 4 minutes. Remove the pot from the burner and set aside.
2. Peel the potatoes and cut into paper-thin slices. Cut the scallions into 1-inch pieces and shred.

3. In a large soup pot, cook the salt pork until it is golden brown. Remove the browned pieces with a slotted spoon and place on a double thickness of paper towels to drain.
4. Drain from the pot all but 2 tablespoons of the pork fat. Add the chopped onion, the thyme, and half the parsley. Cook for 2 or 3 minutes until softened. Pour the fish-cooking liquid into the pot. Add the potatoes, scallions, salt pork, and enough water to cover. Boil until the potatoes are cooked, about 10 minutes.
5. Add the fish, milk, tarragon, and salt and pepper to taste. Heat thoroughly, but don't boil. Ladle the soup into bowls and sprinkle the remaining parsley over the top of each serving.

4–5 SERVINGS

Pat's Tomato Soup

Thick, hot, and hearty, this soup cries for thick slices of Italian bread —
then it's a supper all by itself. It was developed by Pat's mother-in-law, a
farmer's wife, and makes a potful, so leftovers may be frozen for another day.

SOUP INGREDIENTS

1 *peck ripe tomatoes (8 quarts)*
3 *onions*
½ *bunch celery*
7 *sprigs fresh parsley*
7 *whole cloves*
6 *bay leaves*
2 *sprigs fresh basil*

PASTE INGREDIENTS

¾ *cup flour*
½ *cup sugar*
2 *tablespoons salt*
½ *teaspoon freshly ground pepper*
½ *pound butter*

1. Wash the tomatoes, cut into quarters, and chop for 15 seconds in a food processor. In a large soup pot, combine the tomatoes with the onions, celery, parsley, cloves, bay leaves, and basil. Stew for about 2 hours. Put through a food mill or puree in a blender.
2. To make the paste, combine the flour, sugar, salt, pepper, and butter. Add to the tomato mixture and cook until boiling.

5½ QUARTS

Corn and Tomato Soup

They ripen together in the summer, and they make good partners in soup — the South American natives corn and tomatoes. This big batch can be the main dish for supper.

> 2 cups cooked whole kernel corn
> 2 medium tomatoes, chopped
> 4 large stalks celery, chopped
> 1 quart cold water
> 2 tablespoons softened butter
> 3 tablespoons unbleached flour
> 1 cup milk
> ½ cup grated Monterey Jack cheese
> ½ cup chopped pimento
> 2 tablespoons minced fresh oregano
> Salt and freshly ground pepper

1. In a large soup pot, cover the corn, tomatoes, and celery with the cold water. Simmer, covered, for 30 minutes or until the vegetables are tender.
2. In a small saucepan, melt the butter and blend in the flour, making a roux. Gradually add the milk and cook until thickened, stirring frequently. Add the milk mixture to the soup pot and stir well.

3. Add the cheese, pimento, and oregano and stir until the cheese is melted. Add salt and pepper to taste and serve in heated bowls.

2 QUARTS

Zucchini Soup

At some stage of summer, almost every gardener wants to leave zucchinis on other people's doorsteps, ring the bell, and run. Yet the vegetable is so versatile that it can come to the table in a thousand disguises.

> 2 tablespoons butter
> 2 tablespoons extra virgin olive oil
> 1 medium zucchini, chopped and unpeeled (unless skin is tough)
> Salt and freshly ground pepper
> 2 quarts chicken broth, homemade or canned
> ¼ pound spaghettini, uncooked
> 2 medium eggs
> 8 tablespoons grated fresh Romano cheese
> 2 tablespoons grated fresh Parmesan cheese
> 1½ tablespoons chopped fresh parsley
> 1 tablespoon chopped fresh basil

1. Heat the butter and oil in a soup pot, add the zucchini, and cook over medium heat for about 10 minutes. Do not brown. Season with salt and pepper to taste.
2. Add the chicken broth and simmer, covered, for 30 minutes.

3. In the meantime, cook the spaghettini according to the directions on the package until it is al dente. Drain under cool water to stop the cooking and set aside.

4. Whisk the eggs with the two cheeses and the herbs. Add the spaghettini and pour the pasta-and-egg mixture into the soup pot. As soon as the mixture even hints at a simmer, remove it from the burner and give it a whisk. Serve immediately.

6 SERVINGS

The flavors of basil and parsley blend well.

Tofu Soup

The Chinese often eat their soup last, and many times it's a hearty concoction. This one is simple, perfect as an appetizer or as a stand-alone for lunch.

1 tablespoon Chinese tree ears
2 pounds soft tofu
6 cups chicken broth
2 scallions, cut in 1-inch pieces and shredded
2 carrots, peeled and coarsely grated
1½ tablespoons light soy sauce
8 shiitake mushrooms, thinly sliced
Freshly ground black pepper
¼ cup sherry
¼ cup chopped fresh cilantro

1. Soak the tree ears in a bowl of warm water until expanded and soft, about 25 minutes.
2. Slice the tofu and cut into cubes. Drain the tree ears and rinse. Remove the hard stems and shred.
3. Bring the broth to a boil in a saucepan, adding the scallions, carrots, soy sauce, mushrooms, tree ears, and pepper to taste. Simmer for 8 minutes, or until the mushrooms are cooked.

4. Add the tofu, sherry, and cilantro and reheat almost to a simmer. Serve immediately.

6–8 SERVINGS

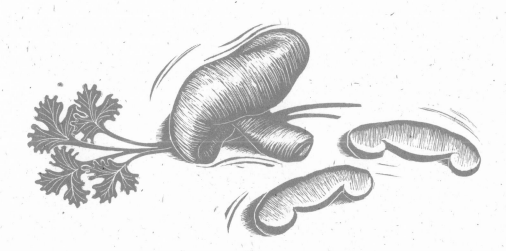

Cock-a-Leekie Soup

This country soup is older than the hills, but not the moors. It comes from Scotland and dates back to Elizabethan times. Cock-a-leekie can be a whole meal when served with a basket of hot baking-powder biscuits or cornbread. You can make it in about an hour.

2½ pounds of boneless, skinless chicken breasts
3 cups water
1 stalk celery, diced
2 carrots, diced
½ cup barley
1 cup chicken broth
2 bay leaves
2 teaspoons minced fresh rosemary
1 teaspoon salt
½ teaspoon freshly ground pepper
¾ pound leeks, white and green parts sliced (about 1½ cups)

1. In a large saucepan, combine the chicken breasts, water, celery, carrots, barley, chicken broth, bay leaves, rosemary, salt, and pepper. Heat to a boil. Reduce the heat, cover, and simmer for about 30 minutes.

2. Add the leeks, heat to a boil, reduce the heat again, and simmer until the chicken is tender.

3. Remove the chicken and let cool. When it is cool enough to handle, cut into bite-size pieces.
4. Skim any fat from the broth and remove the bay leaves. Put the chicken pieces back into the broth and reheat for about 5 minutes.

6 SERVINGS

French Onion Soup

You can spend a couple of hours making this soup, or you can make it in the microwave in about 15 minutes. This is the last-minute method.

> 4 tablespoons butter
> 1 large sweet onion, sliced thin
> 1 large can beef broth (20 ounces)
> 1 garlic clove, minced
> ¼ cup dry white wine
> Salt and freshly ground pepper
> 1½ tablespoons brandy, at room temperature
> Melba toast rounds
> 1 cup shredded Swiss cheese (about ¼ pound)

1. In a three-quart casserole, combine the butter and the separated slices of onion. Cook in the microwave for 3 minutes on high.
2. Stir in the beef broth, garlic, wine, and salt and pepper to taste. Cook in the microwave for 6 minutes on high, turning the casserole and stirring after 3 minutes.

3. Remove the casserole and immediately stir in the brandy. Divide into mugs or bowls and top with Melba toast rounds and shredded cheese.
4. Cook in the microwave for a minute on high to melt the cheese.

4–6 SERVINGS

Rosemary was an ancient remedy for headaches.

Beer and Onion Soup

People across the nation are brewing beer at home, some creating fine, new versions of an age-old drink. Homebrew may be used in this recipe; otherwise use commercial stout.

> *3 large white onions*
> *¼ cup olive oil*
> *Salt and freshly ground pepper*
> *6 cups chicken broth*
> *2 bottles dark beer*
> *3 bay leaves*
> *1 teaspoon minced fresh rosemary*
> *⅛ teaspoon nutmeg*
> *Melba toast or French bread for garnish*

1. Slice the onions as thin as possible. Heat the olive oil in a soup pot and add the onions and the salt and pepper to taste. Cook until onions are light brown, stirring to prevent sticking.
2. Add the chicken broth, beer, bay leaves, rosemary, and nutmeg. Bring to a boil, then reduce the heat and simmer for about 30 minutes. The onions should be soft. Correct the seasonings to taste and remove the bay leaves.
3. Garnish with a slice of Melba toast or a crust of toasted French bread.

6 SERVINGS

Apple Onion Soup

Apple soup doesn't often grace American tables, but Hungarian cooks can vouch for its virtues. This one has the sweetness of cider, the subtle aroma of fresh sage, and the heartiness provided by potatoes.

½ pound potatoes, peeled and cubed (about 1½ cups)
3 medium sweet white onions, peeled and chopped
    (about 1½ cups)
4 medium apples, peeled and coarsely chopped
    (about 3 cups)
2 stalks celery, chopped (about ¾ cup)
2 tablespoons minced fresh sage
2 cups chicken broth
1 cup cider
Salt and freshly ground pepper
1 tablespoon coarsely snipped fresh chives

1. In a soup pot, combine the potatoes, onions, apples, and celery.
2. Mix the sage with the chicken broth and cider and add to the pot. Bring to a boil. Reduce the heat, cover, and simmer for about 30 minutes, or until the potatoes and apples are soft.

3. Put the contents of the pot in a food processor and puree. Return to the pot and reheat. Stir frequently. Season with salt and pepper to taste. Ladle into serving bowls and sprinkle with chives.

4–6 SERVINGS

A bunch of chives hung in a room
was once thought to ward off evil spirits.

Amy's Butternut Squash Soup

Butternut squash are at their best in October, November, and December, when they still have September's flavor and crispness. On a cold day, take the chill off with this hearty soup.

       4 teaspoons butter
   2–3 medium sweet onions, chopped (about 1¼ cups)
       3 medium crisp Cortland or Spy apples,
              chopped (about 2½ cups)
       4 cups butternut squash, peeled and cubed
       3 cups chicken broth
      ¼ teaspoon ground coriander
       1 tablespoon minced fresh sage
      ½ teaspoon freshly ground pepper
       1 cup milk, at room temperature
      ½ teaspoon ground nutmeg
      ½ teaspoon ground cloves

1. Melt the butter over medium-high heat. Add the onions and cook until golden.
2. Add the apples, squash, and broth. Bring to a boil and cover. Reduce the heat and simmer until the squash is tender, about 20 minutes.

3. Put the squash mixture, coriander, sage, and pepper in a food processor and run until smooth. Return the mixture to the pan, and stir in the milk.
4. Cook about 3 minutes to heat through. Pour into bowls and sprinkle with a mixture of nutmeg and cloves.

6 SERVINGS

Matzo Ball Soup

In sickness and in health, a good chicken soup helps make the world go round. And when it's time to make matzo ball soup, the broth is crucial.

MATZO BALLS
3 eggs, separated
½ teaspoon salt
¾ cup matzo meal
1 tablespoon minced fresh parsley
Pinch of cinnamon

1. Beat the egg whites until they stand in soft peaks. Blend in the yolks. Add the salt and matzo meal and refrigerate for at least 20 minutes. The dough will be sticky.
2. Bring a large pot of water to a boil. Form dough into 1-inch balls and drop into the boiling water. Cover, reduce to medium heat, and cook for 45 minutes. Drain.

Soup Ingredients

4- to 5-pound chicken
1 large onion, sliced
4 carrots, cut in half
3 stalks celery, cut into fourths
2 garlic cloves
2 tablespoons chopped fresh parsley
2 teaspoons snipped fresh dill
2 teaspoons salt
Freshly ground pepper

1. In a large soup pot, cover the chicken with water. Bring to a boil, skim off foam, and add the onion, carrots, celery, garlic, parsley, dill, salt, and pepper to taste.
2. Simmer until the chicken is tender, about 2 hours. Strain out the broth and reserve the chicken for another use.
3. Heat the chicken broth in a large pot, add the matzo balls, and heat to a boil. Serve immediately.

6 SERVINGS

Minestrone

It's vegetable soup, the Italian way. Italy, of course, has more ways of preparing it than Rome has hills. Here's one filled with fresh vegetables and herbs, designed to tempt the nose hours before it reaches the palate.

6 tablespoons extra virgin olive oil
2 onions, finely chopped
3 tablespoons chopped fresh parsley
2 garlic cloves, crushed
1 tablespoon chopped fresh thyme
2 tablespoons tomato paste
¼ cup water
3 large tomatoes, peeled, seeded, and chopped
¼ small cabbage, shredded
2 zucchinis, diced
3 carrots, diced
1½ quarts chicken broth
Salt and freshly ground pepper
⅓ cup uncooked rice
1–1½ cups canned white or yellow beans, drained
½ cup grated Parmesan and Romano cheese
2 tablespoons minced fresh parsley

44

1. In a large pot, heat the olive oil and gently cook the onions, parsley, garlic, and thyme until the onions are soft. Thin the tomato paste with ¼ cup water, add to the soup pot, and cook for about 4 minutes.
2. Add the tomatoes, cabbage, zucchinis, carrots, and chicken broth. Season with salt and pepper to taste. Simmer, covered, for about an hour.
3. Bring to a boil, add the rice, and cook until the rice is done. Add the beans and reheat. Mix the grated cheeses with the parsley and sprinkle over each bowl before serving.

10–12 SERVINGS

45

Beanie Bean Soup

Ten kinds of beans can't help but be better than one. This soup has 10 kinds —
that's the amazing part. Some stores sell 10-bean packs so you don't have to fill
your cupboard with half-used packages.

¼ cup each pinto beans, black beans, lima beans,
        red kidney beans, black-eyed peas, navy beans,
        green split and yellow split peas, lentils, and
        garbanzo beans
2 tablespoons barley
2 quarts water
1–2 pounds hot Italian or kielbasa sausage, cut into
        1-inch chunks
1 bay leaf
3 garlic cloves, minced
1 can tomato puree (28 ounces)
2 hot, dried chili peppers, minced
Juice of one large lemon
1 tablespoon chopped fresh marjoram
1⅓ teaspoons chopped fresh thyme
Salt and freshly ground pepper

1. Wash the beans and the barley thoroughly. Place in a pot, cover with water, and soak overnight.
2. In the morning, drain the beans and barley. Add the water, sausage, bay leaf, and garlic. Bring to a boil over high heat. Reduce the heat and simmer for 2½ hours, stirring occasionally.
3. Add the tomato puree, chili peppers, lemon juice, marjoram, thyme, and salt and pepper to taste. Simmer an additional 30 minutes. Remove the bay leaf before serving.

8 SERVINGS

Lemony Cabbage Soup

This is a hearty dish, partly Russian in its ancestry, and it's not hard to imagine a windswept St. Petersburg landscape with men in fur hats and women in heavy scarves bending their heads to avoid the cold. You can make a meal of this on a chilly winter day.

1½ pounds lean beef, cut into 1-inch cubes
2 onions, chopped
2 bay leaves
1 tablespoon chopped fresh marjoram
2 garlic cloves
3 quarts cold water
1 medium head of green cabbage, shredded
4 medium tomatoes, chopped (2 cups)
¼ cup brown sugar
Juice of two lemons
Salt and freshly ground pepper
Plain yogurt for garnish

1. Cover the beef, onions, bay leaves, marjoram, and garlic with the water and simmer, covered, for 1½ hours.
2. Remove the bay leaves. Add the cabbage, tomatoes, sugar, lemon juice, and salt and pepper to taste. Continue to cook until the meat and cabbage are tender, about 30 minutes.
3. The meat may be removed and reserved for another use or left in the soup. Before serving, add a dollop of yogurt to each bowl.

8 SERVINGS

*Bay leaves were made into crowns to honor
ancient poets and heroes.*

Pea Soup

After the baked ham dinner comes the pea soup, this time flavored with fresh oregano.

½ cup dried split peas
4 cups water
1 hambone
1 medium onion, chopped
1 tablespoon minced fresh
    oregano

2 tablespoons butter
1 tablespoon flour
Salt and freshly ground pepper
1 cup milk or light cream, warmed
2 tablespoons chopped fresh
    curly parsley

1. Cover the peas with cold water and soak several hours or overnight.
2. Rinse the peas. Add the water, ham bone, onion, and oregano. Simmer 3 hours or until the peas are soft.
3. Puree the soup mixture in a food processor or blender.
4. In a small pan, melt the butter and stir in the flour until smooth. Return the soup mixture to the pot and stir in the butter and flour mixture. Add salt and pepper to taste.
5. Add the milk or light cream and reheat just short of boiling. Garnish with the parsley.

6–8 SERVINGS

Lime Soup

The ingredients may sound like a gathering of misfits, but they accommodate each other nicely in a soup that lightly introduces a meal.

> 5 cups clear chicken broth
> 1 small garlic clove, peeled
> 2–3 tablespoons light brown sugar
> ¼ cup finely chopped fresh parsley
> Juice of 3 medium limes (about ⅓ cup)
> Salt and freshly ground pepper

1. In a medium saucepan, bring the broth to a boil. Stick a toothpick into the garlic clove (for easy removal later) and add to the broth. Add the sugar and parsley. Simmer for 10 to 15 minutes.
2. Remove from heat and stir in the lime juice. Add salt and pepper to taste. Let stand for at least an hour.
3. Remove the garlic clove. The soup may be reheated or chilled and served cold.

6–8 SERVINGS

Gazpacho

When in Spain, try the regional variations on this theme, especially the smooth, Andalusian version. Virtually a salad in a bowl, gazpacho quickly changed from being a stranger to being on everyone's menu in our own country. Fresh vegetables are important here.

Soup Ingredients

3 tomatoes, peeled
1 garlic clove
1 sweet white onion, cut into small chunks
1 green pepper, seeded and quartered
1 tablespoon chopped fresh basil
⅛ teaspoon cayenne
¼ cup white wine vinegar
¼ cup olive oil
¾ cup tomato juice
Freshly ground pepper

Garnishes

1 cucumber, finely chopped
1 small onion, finely chopped
1 green pepper, finely chopped
1 cup croutons

1. To make the soup, liquefy the tomatoes, garlic, onion, green pepper, and basil in a blender. Add the cayenne, vinegar, olive oil, tomato juice, and pepper. Cover and chill for at least 3 hours.
2. To serve, put the garnishes — cucumber, onion, green pepper, and croutons — into chilled soup bowls and pour the very cold soup over them.

6–8 SERVINGS

Bubbie's Borscht

My mother-in-law served this soup with boiled new potatoes, which some family members would pop right into the chilled soup. That provided not only the taste sensation of hot and cold but the contrast of textures as well.

10 large beets, peeled and grated
Handful of beet greens, coarsely chopped
2½ quarts water
1 onion, minced
2 garlic cloves, minced
2½ teaspoons salt
2 tablespoons sugar
Juice of two lemons
1 cup sour cream or plain yogurt
Freshly ground pepper
4 tablespoons snipped fresh chives

1. Combine beets, greens, water, onion, garlic, and salt in a soup pot. Bring to a boil, reduce the heat, and simmer for about an hour.
2. Add the sugar and lemon juice. Cook for another 10 minutes and correct the seasoning. Chill.

3. Pour into chilled bowls, add a dollop of sour cream or yogurt, and sprinkle with pepper to taste and chives.

8 SERVINGS

Summer Carrot Soup

When carrots are fresh from the garden and so much sweeter than in midwinter, take the time — only 20 minutes — to make this soup. Then, let it cool for a couple of hours before serving.

6–8 *fresh carrots, diced (about 3 cups)*
2 *scallions, slivered (about ¼ cup)*
1 *small celery stalk, chopped*
1 *teaspoon snipped fresh dill*
3 *cups chicken broth*
Salt and freshly ground pepper
½ *cup plain yogurt*
3 *tablespoons finely snipped fresh chives*

1. In a saucepan, cook the carrots, scallions, celery, and dill in the chicken broth until the vegetables are tender. Set aside to cool.
2. Puree the cooled mixture and add salt and pepper to taste.
3. Pour the soup into a covered glass or plastic container (not metal) and chill for at least 2 hours before serving.
4. To serve, top each bowl with a dollop of yogurt and sprinkle with chives.

4–6 SERVINGS

Salad Soup

Salad vegetables may look limp and unlovely after dinner, but they don't have to be thrown away. Forget the guilt trip and make soup.

> 4 cups leftover dressed salad
> 1 cup buttermilk
> 1½ cups plain yogurt
> ¼ cup sour cream
> 1 tablespoon lemon juice
> 2 garlic cloves
> 2 tablespoons minced fresh basil
> 6 tablespoons water
> Salt and freshly ground pepper
> 2 medium tomatoes, diced (1 cup)

1. Place the salad, buttermilk, yogurt, sour cream, lemon juice, garlic, basil, and water in a blender or food processor and puree until smooth. Season with salt and pepper to taste.
2. Pour into a large serving bowl and stir in the diced tomatoes. Serve chilled.

3–4 SERVINGS

Mint represents virtue.

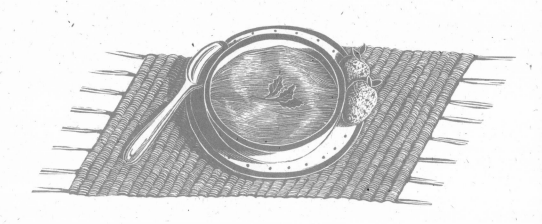

Chilled Strawberry Soup

An ice-cold fruit soup in a chilled bowl tames the heat of July. Look for strawberries that are ripe but firm. If you're picking the berries yourself, harvest them
in the afternoon when they've gained sweetness from the sun.

> 1 *quart fresh strawberries*
> 1 *cup sugar*
> 1 *cup plain yogurt*
> 2 *teaspoons minced fresh mint*
> 4 *cups ice water*
> ¾ *cup dry white wine*

1. Chop the strawberries in a food processor and then force them through a
   sieve. Mix in the sugar, yogurt, and mint.
2. Add the ice water and white wine and sample for sweetness. Chill for at
   least 2 hours before serving.

8 SERVINGS

Frosty Melon Soup

For this soup, consider using glass bowls, chilled until they are frosted. Filled with pale green soup, they offer up a real cooler on a hot summer's day.

> 6 cups water
> 1 carrot, peeled and halved
> ½ teaspoon celery seeds
> 1 bay leaf
> 3 teaspoons minced fresh lemon thyme
> 1½-inch piece of fresh ginger root
> 1 honeydew melon
> Salt
> Juice of 3 limes
> Slim spirals of lime peel

1. In a large saucepan, bring the water to a boil. Add the carrot, celery seeds, bay leaf, and lemon thyme. Cover, reduce the heat, and simmer for 30 minutes.
2. Strain the broth and return to the pot. Peel and shred the ginger root. Add to the pot and simmer for 15 minutes.

3. Quarter the melon, remove seeds, and peel. Cut into chunks. Place in a food processor or blender with about 1 cup of the broth and process to a smooth puree. Stir the puree into the remaining broth. Season with salt to taste. Refrigerate, covered, for at least 3 hours.
4. Just before serving, stir in the lime juice. Serve garnished with the lime peel.

4 SERVINGS

Index

Converting Recipe Measurements to Metric

Use the following formulas for converting U.S. measurements to metric. Since the conversions are not exact, it's important to convert the measurements for all of the ingredients to maintain the same proportions as the original recipe.

WHEN THE MEASUREMENT GIVEN IS	MULTIPLY IT BY	TO CONVERT TO
teaspoons	4.93	milliliters
tablespoons	14.79	milliliters
fluid ounces	29.57	milliliters
cups (liquid)	236.59	milliliters
cups (liquid)	.236	liters
cups (dry)	275.31	milliliters
cups (dry)	.275	liters
pints (liquid)	473.18	milliliters
pints (liquid)	.473	liters
pints (dry)	550.61	milliliters
pints (dry)	.551	liters
quarts (liquid)	946.36	milliliters
quarts (liquid)	.946	liters
quarts (dry)	1101.22	milliliters
quarts (dry)	1.101	liters
gallons	3.785	liters
ounces	28.35	grams
pounds	.454	kilograms
inches	2.54	centimeters
degrees Fahrenheit	$5/9$ (temperature − 32)	degrees Celsius

While standard metric measurements for dry ingredients are given as units of mass, U.S. measurements are given as units of volume. Therefore, the conversions listed above for dry ingredients are given in the metric equivalent of volume.